Think Positive

Paul Saulivan

Table of Contents

INTRODUCTION

In a world often dominated by extremes—where relentless positivity can sometimes feel obligatory and acknowledging challenges can be seen as pessimistic—there exists a nuanced approach to navigating life's complexities: realistic optimism. This mindset isn't about blind positivity or ignoring difficulties; rather, it's a balanced perspective that integrates hopefulness with a pragmatic understanding of reality.

Realistic optimism encourages us to acknowledge both the opportunities and obstacles in our paths, while maintaining confidence in our ability to overcome challenges. It's grounded in psychological principles that emphasize resilience, adaptive thinking, and emotional well-being. By embracing realistic optimism, individuals can cultivate a mindset that fosters personal growth, enhances resilience, and improves overall life satisfaction.

This book explores the multifaceted nature of realistic optimism, delving into its psychological underpinnings, practical applications in everyday life, and the science-backed benefits it offers.

CHAPTER ONE

The Limitations of Traditional Positive Thinking

In this opening chapter, we explore the foundational principles of traditional positive thinking and its pervasive influence in modern culture. While positive thinking has its merits, we delve into its limitations and how an overly optimistic mindset can sometimes lead to unrealistic expectations and disappointment.

Positive thinking has been widely promoted as a panacea for personal growth and happiness, promising that maintaining a sunny outlook will lead to success, resilience, and fulfillment. While there is merit in cultivating optimism, it's essential to recognize the inherent limitations of traditional positive thinking.

The Promise and Pitfalls

Traditional positive thinking advocates believe in the power of thoughts to shape reality. They emphasize the importance of maintaining a positive attitude at all costs, suggesting that optimism alone can overcome adversity and attract desired outcomes. This perspective often resonates in motivational speeches, self-help literature, and pop psychology, where phrases like "think positive" and "visualize success" abound.

Indeed, there is evidence to suggest that a positive mindset can improve mood, boost motivation, and enhance overall well-being. Studies in positive psychology have shown correlations between optimism and resilience, suggesting that those who approach challenges with a positive outlook may recover more quickly from setbacks.

When Positive Thinking Falls Short

However, the limitations of traditional positive thinking become evident when faced with complex and challenging situations. Life is not always predictable or controllable, and maintaining unwavering positivity can sometimes feel unrealistic or even dismissive of genuine struggles. For example, when confronted with significant setbacks such as job loss, illness, or relationship breakdown, urging someone to "stay positive" can seem insensitive or superficial.

Moreover, the pressure to stay positive can lead to feelings of guilt or self-blame when individuals find it challenging to maintain an optimistic outlook in the face of adversity. This can create a cycle where individuals feel inadequate or ashamed for experiencing normal human emotions like sadness, fear, or anger.

Embracing Reality: Why Honest Assessment Matters

A crucial aspect missing from traditional positive thinking is a balanced view of reality. Honest assessment involves acknowledging both the positive and negative aspects of a situation, allowing individuals to make informed decisions and take appropriate actions. This approach is rooted in emotional intelligence, where recognizing and processing emotions—both positive and negative—is essential for personal growth and resilience.

By embracing reality, individuals can develop a deeper understanding of themselves and their circumstances. They can cultivate resilience by learning from setbacks and adapting their strategies accordingly. This process fosters a more authentic sense of self-confidence and optimism that is grounded in real-world experiences rather than wishful thinking.

Moving Forward: Towards Realistic Optimism

Recognizing the limitations of traditional positive thinking paves the way for a more nuanced approach known as realistic optimism. Realistic optimism encourages a positive outlook while acknowledging the complexities of life. It recognizes that challenges and setbacks are inevitable but believes in one's ability to navigate through them effectively.

Unlike traditional positive thinking, which may gloss over difficulties in favor of a cheerful facade, realistic optimism encourages individuals to confront challenges head-on. It involves setting realistic goals, developing effective problem-solving skills, and seeking support when needed— all while maintaining a hopeful attitude grounded in practicality and resilience.

In the chapters that follow, we will explore how to cultivate realistic optimism in various aspects of life, from relationships and goal-setting to personal growth and well-being. By understanding its limitations, we can embrace a mindset that promotes genuine growth, resilience, and lasting happiness.

CHAPTER TWO

Introducing Realistic Optimism

Here, we introduce the concept of realistic optimism as a balanced approach that combines positivity with a realistic assessment of circumstances. We discuss how realistic optimists maintain a hopeful outlook while acknowledging challenges and setbacks, fostering resilience and a healthier mindset.

In a world where the allure of unwavering positivity often overshadows the complexities of real-life experiences, realistic optimism emerges as a balanced and pragmatic approach to navigating the ups and downs of existence. This chapter delves into the essence of realistic optimism, contrasting it with traditional positive thinking and exploring its profound implications for personal development and emotional resilience.

What is Realistic Optimism?

Realistic optimism is more than just a mindset; it's a philosophy that blends optimism with a clear-eyed view of reality. Unlike the sometimes superficial cheerfulness of traditional positive thinking, which might overlook challenges or dismiss genuine concerns, realistic optimism encourages individuals to acknowledge and embrace both the possibilities and limitations inherent in any situation.

At its core, realistic optimism recognizes that life is inherently unpredictable. It acknowledges that setbacks, disappointments, and obstacles are natural parts of the human experience. However, instead of succumbing to pessimism or resignation, realistic optimists maintain a hopeful outlook. They believe in their capacity to overcome adversity, learn from setbacks, and grow stronger in the process.

The Power of Balanced Expectations

One of the key tenets of realistic optimism is the importance of setting balanced expectations. While traditional positive thinking might encourage setting lofty goals without considering potential obstacles, realistic optimism encourages individuals to set goals that are challenging yet attainable. This approach fosters motivation and resilience by preparing individuals for the inevitable setbacks while maintaining a sense of hope and determination.

Balanced expectations also enable realistic optimists to approach decisions and challenges with clarity and pragmatism. By realistically assessing risks and uncertainties, individuals can make informed choices and take proactive steps to achieve their goals. This proactive mindset is crucial for personal growth and success in both professional and personal spheres.

Finding Strength in Realism and Hope

Contrary to the misconception that realism and optimism are mutually exclusive, realistic optimism demonstrates how these seemingly contradictory qualities can complement each other. Realism provides a solid foundation of understanding and acceptance, allowing individuals to face challenges with courage and resilience. Meanwhile, optimism fuels hope and perseverance, empowering individuals to pursue their aspirations and dreams despite obstacles.

Finding strength in realism and hope involves cultivating a mindset that balances proactive planning with flexibility and adaptability. It encourages individuals to learn from past experiences, anticipate potential challenges, and embrace opportunities for growth and learning. By embracing both realism and hope, individuals can navigate life's uncertainties with confidence and grace.

Practical Strategies for Cultivating Realistic Optimism

Cultivating realistic optimism is a gradual and ongoing process that involves intentional effort and self-reflection. This chapter explores practical strategies and techniques for developing a realistic optimistic mindset:

- **Mindful Awareness:** Practicing mindfulness allows individuals to observe their thoughts and emotions without judgment. This awareness enables realistic optimists to recognize negative thought patterns and reframe them in a more constructive light.

- **Goal Setting and Planning:** Setting realistic goals and developing actionable plans are essential components of realistic optimism. By breaking down larger goals into smaller, achievable steps, individuals can maintain motivation and track progress effectively.

- **Building Resilience:** Resilience is the ability to bounce back from setbacks and challenges. Realistic optimists cultivate resilience by viewing failures as opportunities for growth, seeking support from others, and maintaining a positive outlook even in difficult times.

- **Practicing Gratitude:** Gratitude is a powerful antidote to negativity and pessimism. Regularly acknowledging and appreciating the positive aspects of life can help individuals maintain a balanced perspective and enhance overall well-being.

- **Seeking Perspective:** Realistic optimists recognize the value of seeking perspective from others, whether through mentorship, peer support, or professional guidance. Engaging with diverse viewpoints can provide new insights and solutions to overcome obstacles.

In conclusion, realistic optimism offers a refreshing alternative to traditional positive thinking by encouraging individuals to embrace both optimism and realism in equal measure. By cultivating a mindset that acknowledges challenges while maintaining hope and determination, individuals can navigate life's uncertainties with resilience, grace, and a genuine sense of optimism. In the following chapters, we will explore how to apply these principles of realistic optimism to various aspects of life, from relationships and career to personal growth and well-being.

CHAPTER THREE

Embracing the Full Spectrum of Emotions

This chapter challenges the notion that positivity should dominate our emotional landscape. We explore the importance of embracing a full range of emotions, including so-called "negative" emotions, and how this authenticity contributes to emotional intelligence and well-being.

In a culture that often emphasizes positivity and happiness as the ultimate goals, the full range of human emotions—both pleasant and unpleasant—can be overlooked or undervalued. This chapter explores the importance of embracing and understanding the entirety of our emotional landscape, highlighting how this approach contributes to psychological well-being, authenticity, and resilience.

The Myth of Constant Positivity

Society often promotes the idea that happiness and positivity should be the default emotional states. This notion can create unrealistic expectations and pressures for individuals to suppress or deny emotions perceived as negative, such as sadness, anger, fear, or anxiety. The consequence is a disconnection from our authentic selves and a reluctance to acknowledge and process genuine feelings.

Understanding Negative Emotions

Contrary to common belief, negative emotions serve essential functions in our lives. They provide valuable information about our needs, desires, and boundaries. For example, feelings of sadness may signal a need for reflection or comfort, while anger might indicate a perceived injustice or boundary violation. By understanding and accepting these emotions, individuals can respond to them in constructive ways that promote emotional health and resilience.

Healthy Ways to Navigate Emotions

Rather than striving to eliminate negative emotions, a healthier approach involves learning to navigate them effectively. This chapter explores strategies for managing emotions in productive ways:

- **Mindfulness and Emotional Awareness:** Practicing mindfulness allows individuals to observe their emotions without judgment, fostering a deeper understanding of their triggers and patterns.
- **Emotional Regulation Techniques:** Techniques such as deep breathing, progressive muscle relaxation, and cognitive reframing can help individuals regulate intense emotions and maintain emotional balance.

- **Expressive Writing and Art Therapy:** Engaging in creative activities like writing or art can provide a safe outlet for expressing and processing emotions that may be difficult to verbalize.
- **Seeking Support:** Sharing emotions with trusted friends, family members, or mental health professionals can provide validation, empathy, and practical guidance for coping with challenging emotions.

Challenging Toxic Positivity

Toxic positivity refers to the overemphasis on maintaining a positive outlook at all costs, even when it dismisses or invalidates genuine feelings of distress or discomfort. This chapter examines the harmful effects of toxic positivity and encourages individuals to cultivate a more balanced perspective that acknowledges both the joys and challenges of life.

Developing Emotional Resilience

Emotional resilience is the ability to adapt to adversity and bounce back from setbacks. Embracing the full spectrum of emotions is essential for developing resilience, as it allows individuals to learn from difficult experiences, build coping skills, and maintain a sense of hope and optimism amidst adversity.

Practices for Cultivating Emotional Well-being

This chapter concludes with practical exercises and recommendations for cultivating emotional well-being:

- **Daily Emotional Check-ins:** Take time each day to reflect on your emotions and identify any patterns or recurring themes.
- **Journaling:** Keep a journal to track your emotions, write about significant events, and

explore your thoughts and feelings in a safe space.

- **Self-Compassion:** Practice self-compassion by treating yourself with kindness and understanding during times of emotional distress.

- **Mindful Listening:** Practice active listening and empathy in your interactions with others, creating a supportive environment for emotional expression.

In conclusion, embracing the full spectrum of emotions is essential for authentic living, psychological resilience, and overall well-being. By acknowledging and understanding both the positive and negative aspects of our emotional experiences, individuals can cultivate deeper self-awareness, healthier relationships, and a greater capacity for navigating life's challenges with grace and resilience.

CHAPTER FOUR

Cultivating Resilience through Adversity

Resilience is a key component of realistic optimism. We examine how setbacks and failures can be valuable learning opportunities, and we provide practical strategies for building resilience that empower individuals to bounce back stronger from adversity.

Resilience is not merely bouncing back from adversity but growing stronger and wiser in the process. This chapter delves into the essential components of resilience and provides practical strategies for cultivating this crucial trait in the face of life's challenges.

Understanding Resilience

Resilience is the ability to adapt and thrive in the face of adversity, setbacks, or trauma. It involves psychological toughness, emotional strength, and the capacity to recover and learn from difficult experiences. Resilience is not innate but can be developed and strengthened through intentional practices and mindset shifts.

Learning from Setbacks and Failures

One of the core elements of resilience is the ability to learn and grow from setbacks and failures. This chapter explores how reframing setbacks as opportunities for learning and growth can empower individuals to overcome obstacles and emerge stronger. By adopting a growth mindset—a belief that abilities and intelligence can be developed through dedication and hard work—individuals can approach challenges with resilience and determination.

The Role of Resilience in Realistic Optimism

Resilience and realistic optimism go hand in hand. While realistic optimism fosters a positive outlook grounded in a realistic assessment of circumstances, resilience provides the strength and endurance to persevere when faced with adversity. Together, these qualities form a powerful foundation for navigating life's uncertainties with grace and courage.

Strategies for Building Resilience

This chapter provides practical strategies and exercises for building resilience:

- **Cognitive Restructuring:** Challenge negative thought patterns and develop more adaptive ways of thinking that promote resilience and optimism.
- **Strengthening Social Connections:** Cultivate supportive relationships with friends, family, and community members

who can provide emotional support and encouragement during challenging times.

- **Self-Care Practices:** Prioritize self-care activities such as exercise, adequate sleep, healthy nutrition, and relaxation techniques to enhance physical and emotional resilience.

- **Mindfulness and Stress Reduction:** Practice mindfulness meditation and stress reduction techniques to cultivate present-moment awareness and develop coping skills for managing stress.

- **Seeking Meaning and Purpose:** Reflect on personal values and goals to find meaning and purpose in difficult experiences, which can foster resilience and psychological well-being.

Building Resilience in Children and Adolescents

Resilience is a valuable trait that can be nurtured from a young age. This chapter explores strategies for promoting resilience in children and adolescents, including fostering positive relationships, teaching problem-solving skills, and encouraging emotional expression and coping strategies.

Case Studies and Examples

Illustrative case studies and real-life examples demonstrate how individuals have cultivated resilience in the face of adversity. These stories highlight resilience as a dynamic and evolving process that involves setbacks, growth, and personal transformation.

In conclusion, cultivating resilience through adversity is a transformative journey that involves embracing challenges, learning from setbacks, and developing adaptive coping strategies. By integrating resilience-building practices into daily life, individuals can strengthen their capacity to thrive in the face of adversity and emerge more resilient, confident, and empowered.

CHAPTER FIVE

Honesty and Authenticity in Self-Talk

Here, we critique the concept of toxic positivity and emphasize the importance of honest and authentic self-talk. By fostering a compassionate inner dialogue that acknowledges both strengths and weaknesses, individuals can cultivate genuine self-confidence and self-awareness.

Self-talk, the ongoing internal dialogue we have with ourselves, plays a pivotal role in shaping our beliefs, emotions, and behaviors. This chapter explores the importance of cultivating honesty and authenticity in our self-talk, challenging the prevalent narratives of toxic positivity and encouraging a more balanced and compassionate inner dialogue.

Understanding Self-Talk

Self-talk encompasses the thoughts and beliefs we consciously or unconsciously repeat to ourselves throughout the day. It can be supportive and empowering, fostering confidence and motivation, or it can be critical and undermining, contributing to self-doubt and negativity. Understanding the impact of self-talk is crucial as it influences our perceptions of ourselves, others, and the world around us.

The Myth of Toxic Positivity

Toxic positivity refers to the tendency to maintain a positive outlook at all costs, often dismissing or invalidating genuine emotions and experiences. In the context of self-talk, toxic positivity manifests as an inner dialogue that denies or suppresses difficult emotions, pressures oneself to "stay positive," and imposes unrealistic expectations for happiness and success.

Challenging Toxic Self-Talk

This chapter encourages individuals to identify and challenge toxic self-talk by:

- **Recognizing Negative Patterns:** Developing awareness of recurring negative thoughts and beliefs that contribute to self-limiting beliefs and emotional distress.
- **Cognitive Restructuring:** Engaging in cognitive restructuring techniques to challenge and reframe negative self-talk into more balanced and realistic perspectives.
- **Practicing Self-Compassion:** Cultivating self-compassion involves treating oneself with kindness and understanding, particularly during moments of self-criticism or failure.
- **Embracing Imperfection:** Embracing imperfection and acknowledging that setbacks and mistakes are natural parts of the human experience.

Developing Honest and Authentic Self-Talk

Authentic self-talk involves cultivating a compassionate and truthful inner dialogue that acknowledges both strengths and weaknesses. It encourages individuals to:

- **Acknowledge and Validate Emotions:** Recognizing and validating a full range of emotions, including difficult ones like sadness, anger, or fear, without judgment.
- **Celebrate Achievements:** Acknowledging accomplishments and strengths, no matter how small, to build self-confidence and self-esteem.
- **Setting Realistic Expectations:** Setting realistic expectations for oneself and recognizing that growth and progress take time and effort.
- **Seeking Support:** Seeking support from trusted friends, family members, or mental

health professionals to process difficult emotions and gain perspective.

The Power of Affirmations and Positive Self-Talk

Positive self-talk involves using affirmations and supportive statements to promote self-belief, motivation, and resilience. This chapter explores effective techniques for:

- **Creating Affirmations:** Developing personalized affirmations that reflect specific goals, values, and aspirations.
- **Repetition and Consistency:** Practicing affirmations consistently to reinforce positive beliefs and counteract negative self-talk.
- **Visualization:** Using visualization techniques to mentally rehearse success scenarios and strengthen belief in one's abilities.

Case Studies and Personal Narratives

Throughout this chapter, case studies and personal narratives illustrate the transformative power of cultivating honesty and authenticity in self-talk. These stories highlight individuals' journeys to overcome self-limiting beliefs, embrace vulnerability, and cultivate a more compassionate and empowering inner dialogue.

In conclusion, honing honesty and authenticity in self-talk is essential for cultivating resilience, self-compassion, and emotional well-being. By challenging toxic positivity, embracing imperfection, and practicing self-compassion, individuals can foster a more balanced and supportive inner dialogue that promotes growth, confidence, and authentic living. The following chapters will continue to explore practical strategies for integrating these principles into various aspects of life, including relationships, goal-setting, and personal growth.

CHAPTER SIX

Relationships and Realistic Expectations

Realistic optimism extends beyond individual mindset to interpersonal dynamics. We explore how managing expectations in relationships, setting boundaries, and nurturing authentic connections can enhance overall well-being and fulfillment.

Relationships are fundamental to our well-being, yet they can also be sources of stress and disappointment when our expectations are unrealistic. This chapter explores the dynamics of relationships through the lens of realistic expectations, emphasizing the importance of communication, empathy, and mutual understanding in fostering healthy connections.

Understanding Relationship Expectations

Expectations in relationships encompass our beliefs and desires about how others should behave, communicate, and respond to us. While expectations can serve as guidelines for healthy interactions, unrealistic or uncommunicated expectations can lead to misunderstandings, conflicts, and dissatisfaction.

The Impact of Unrealistic Expectations

Unrealistic expectations in relationships can manifest in various ways:

- **Idealization vs. Reality:** Expecting perfection or viewing others through an idealized lens can set unrealistic standards that no one can meet.
- **Unspoken Assumptions:** Assuming that others should intuitively understand our needs and desires without clear

communication can lead to frustration and disappointment.

- **Comparison Trap:** Comparing our relationships to idealized portrayals in media or others' seemingly perfect relationships can create feelings of inadequacy or dissatisfaction.

Embracing Realistic Expectations

This chapter advocates for embracing realistic expectations in relationships, which involves:

- **Clear Communication:** Communicating openly and honestly about expectations, boundaries, and needs fosters mutual understanding and reduces misunderstandings.
- **Flexibility and Adaptability:** Recognizing that relationships evolve over time and may require adjustments in expectations based on

changing circumstances or individual growth.

- **Respect for Differences:** Acknowledging and respecting differences in personalities, communication styles, and preferences promotes empathy and strengthens relationships.

Setting Healthy Boundaries

Healthy boundaries are essential for maintaining respectful and fulfilling relationships. This chapter explores strategies for:

- **Identifying Boundaries:** Identifying personal boundaries related to time, space, emotions, and values.
- **Communicating Boundaries:** Clearly communicating boundaries to others in a respectful and assertive manner.
- **Respecting Others' Boundaries:** Respecting the boundaries of others and

recognizing that boundaries contribute to mutual respect and trust.

Navigating Conflict and Resolution

Conflict is a natural part of relationships and can provide opportunities for growth and understanding. This chapter discusses effective strategies for:

- **Conflict Resolution:** Approaching conflicts with empathy, active listening, and a willingness to compromise.
- **Seeking Understanding:** Striving to understand others' perspectives and emotions during conflicts promotes empathy and strengthens emotional bonds.

Cultivating Empathy and Compassion

Empathy and compassion are foundational to nurturing meaningful connections. This chapter explores:

- **Empathetic Listening:** Practicing active listening and validating others' emotions and experiences.

- **Offering Support:** Providing emotional support and practical assistance during challenging times strengthens bonds and fosters trust.

Case Studies and Real-Life Examples

Throughout this chapter, case studies and real-life examples illustrate the impact of realistic expectations on various types of relationships, including romantic partnerships, friendships, family dynamics, and professional relationships. These stories highlight the importance of communication, empathy, and mutual respect in fostering healthy and fulfilling connections.

In conclusion, embracing realistic expectations in relationships is essential for promoting mutual understanding, respect, and emotional well-being.

By communicating openly, setting healthy boundaries, and cultivating empathy, individuals can build strong and resilient relationships that contribute to their overall happiness and fulfillment. The following chapters will continue to explore practical strategies for applying these principles to personal growth, goal-setting, and emotional resilience.

CHAPTER SEVEN

Achieving Goals with Realistic Planning

Setting realistic goals is essential for sustainable growth and success. We discuss effective goal-setting strategies, the importance of creating actionable plans, and how to adapt goals based on changing circumstances to maintain motivation and progress.

Setting goals is essential for personal growth and success, but achieving them requires more than just optimism—it requires realistic planning and strategic execution. This chapter explores the principles of goal-setting, realistic planning, and effective strategies for turning aspirations into tangible achievements.

The Importance of Goal-Setting

Goals provide direction, motivation, and a sense of purpose in life. Whether they are short-term or long-term, personal or professional, goals help individuals focus their efforts and resources toward desired outcomes. However, setting goals without realistic planning can lead to frustration and setbacks.

Understanding Realistic Planning

Realistic planning involves setting achievable goals based on a thorough assessment of resources, capabilities, and potential obstacles. It requires:

- **Clarity and Specificity:** Clearly defining goals with measurable outcomes and timelines.
- **Assessment of Resources:** Evaluating available resources, such as time, skills, knowledge, and support networks, needed to achieve the goals.

- **Identification of Potential Obstacles:** Anticipating challenges or barriers that may hinder progress and developing contingency plans.

Strategies for Effective Goal Achievement

This chapter explores practical strategies for achieving goals through realistic planning:

- **SMART Goals:** Setting goals that are Specific, Measurable, Achievable, Relevant, and Time-bound (SMART) ensures clarity and focus.
- **Breakdown of Goals:** Breaking down larger goals into smaller, manageable tasks and milestones enhances motivation and progress tracking.
- **Prioritization:** Prioritizing tasks based on urgency and importance helps individuals allocate time and resources effectively.

- **Time Management:** Using time management techniques, such as setting deadlines, scheduling tasks, and minimizing distractions, enhances productivity and goal attainment.

Adapting Goals and Flexibility

Flexibility is key to realistic planning. This chapter discusses:

- **Adaptation to Change:** Being open to adjusting goals and strategies based on evolving circumstances or new information.
- **Learning from Setbacks:** Viewing setbacks as learning opportunities and adjusting plans accordingly fosters resilience and persistence.
- **Celebrating Milestones:** Celebrating achievements and milestones along the way boosts morale and maintains motivation.

Accountability and Support

Accountability and support play crucial roles in goal achievement. This chapter explores:

- **Accountability Partners:** Engaging with accountability partners or mentors who provide encouragement, feedback, and accountability.
- **Seeking Support:** Seeking support from friends, family, or professionals who can offer guidance, expertise, and practical assistance.

Case Studies and Examples

Throughout this chapter, case studies and real-life examples illustrate successful goal achievement through realistic planning. These stories highlight individuals who have applied effective strategies, overcome obstacles, and achieved significant milestones in various domains, including career advancement, personal development, and health and wellness.

In conclusion, achieving goals requires more than wishful thinking—it requires realistic planning, strategic execution, and perseverance. By setting SMART goals, breaking them down into manageable tasks, and adapting plans as needed, individuals can enhance their chances of success and fulfillment. The following chapters will continue to explore practical strategies for applying realistic optimism to other aspects of life, including personal growth, relationships, and emotional resilience.

CHAPTER EIGHT

Mindfulness and Acceptance

Mindfulness practices are integral to realistic optimism, enabling individuals to stay grounded in the present moment and accept things as they are without judgment. We explore mindfulness techniques that cultivate inner peace and resilience in the face of uncertainty.

Mindfulness and acceptance are powerful practices that promote emotional resilience, self-awareness, and overall well-being. This chapter explores the principles of mindfulness and acceptance, their benefits, and practical strategies for integrating these practices into daily life.

Understanding Mindfulness

Mindfulness is the practice of being present and fully engaged in the present moment, without judgment. It involves paying attention to thoughts, feelings, sensations, and the surrounding environment with openness and curiosity. Mindfulness encourages individuals to observe their experiences without reacting impulsively or getting caught up in automatic patterns of thinking.

Benefits of Mindfulness

Research has shown that mindfulness offers numerous benefits for mental, emotional, and physical health, including:

- **Stress Reduction:** Mindfulness practices such as meditation and deep breathing can reduce stress levels and promote relaxation.
- **Improved Focus and Attention:** Regular mindfulness practice enhances cognitive function, attentional control, and the ability to sustain focus on tasks.

- **Emotional Regulation:** Mindfulness cultivates awareness of emotions and helps individuals respond to them in constructive ways, reducing emotional reactivity and enhancing emotional resilience.
- **Enhanced Well-being:** Mindfulness contributes to a greater sense of overall well-being, increased self-awareness, and improved relationships with others.

Practical Strategies for Cultivating Mindfulness

This chapter explores practical techniques for incorporating mindfulness into daily life:

- **Mindful Breathing:** Engaging in deep breathing exercises to center oneself and cultivate present-moment awareness.
- **Body Scan Meditation:** Practicing body scan meditation to observe physical sensations and promote relaxation and body awareness.

- **Mindful Eating:** Paying attention to the sensory experiences of eating, such as taste, texture, and aroma, without distractions.
- **Walking Meditation:** Practicing walking meditation to focus on each step and cultivate mindfulness while moving.

Understanding Acceptance

Acceptance is the practice of acknowledging and embracing one's thoughts, feelings, and experiences without resistance or judgment. It involves:

- **Radical Acceptance:** Embracing reality as it is, including both pleasant and unpleasant experiences, without attempting to change or control them.
- **Self-Compassion:** Treating oneself with kindness and understanding during difficult times, acknowledging imperfections, and learning from mistakes.

- **Letting Go of Control:** Releasing the need to control outcomes and embracing uncertainty as a natural part of life.

Benefits of Acceptance

Acceptance fosters emotional resilience and psychological well-being by:

- **Reducing Inner Conflict:** Accepting reality reduces inner turmoil and resistance to difficult emotions, promoting inner peace and equanimity.
- **Enhancing Adaptability:** Acceptance allows individuals to adapt more flexibly to changing circumstances and navigate life's challenges with greater ease.
- **Improving Relationships:** Accepting oneself and others fosters empathy, compassion, and deeper connections in relationships.

Integrating Mindfulness and Acceptance

This chapter discusses how mindfulness and acceptance complement each other:

- **Mindful Acceptance:** Using mindfulness to observe and accept thoughts, emotions, and experiences without judgment or attachment.
- **Mindful Self-Compassion:** Cultivating self-compassion through mindfulness practices to offer oneself kindness and understanding during moments of difficulty.

Case Studies and Examples

Throughout this chapter, case studies and real-life examples illustrate how individuals have benefited from mindfulness and acceptance practices. These stories highlight personal transformations, improved resilience, and enhanced well-being achieved through regular mindfulness meditation, acceptance of self and others, and embracing life's uncertainties.

In conclusion, mindfulness and acceptance are transformative practices that promote emotional resilience, self-awareness, and overall well-being. By incorporating mindfulness techniques and cultivating acceptance into daily life, individuals can enhance their ability to cope with stress, navigate challenges, and foster deeper connections with themselves and others. The following chapters will continue to explore practical applications of these principles in various aspects of life, including personal growth, relationships, and emotional well-being.

CHAPTER NINE

The Science behind Realistic Optimism

Drawing on psychological research and neuroscience, this chapter explores the scientific basis of optimism and its impact on mental and physical health. Case studies and examples illustrate how realistic optimism can lead to better outcomes and enhanced well-being.

Realistic optimism blends a positive outlook with a realistic assessment of challenges, but its efficacy extends beyond philosophy—it's grounded in scientific principles. This chapter explores the scientific foundations of realistic optimism, its psychological underpinnings, and the research-backed benefits it offers for personal well-being and resilience.

Understanding Realistic Optimism

Realistic optimism is a mindset that acknowledges both positive and negative aspects of situations while maintaining hope and confidence in one's ability to navigate challenges effectively. Unlike blind optimism, which may ignore potential obstacles, realistic optimism encourages individuals to approach goals and problems with a balanced perspective.

Psychological Foundations

This chapter delves into the psychological theories and principles that support realistic optimism:

- **Positive Psychology:** Realistic optimism aligns with the principles of positive psychology, which focuses on strengths, virtues, and factors that contribute to a fulfilling life.

- **Cognitive Behavioral Therapy (CBT):** CBT emphasizes the role of thoughts and beliefs in shaping emotions and behaviors. Realistic optimism integrates CBT techniques by encouraging individuals to challenge negative thought patterns and reframe situations in a more positive and realistic light.

- **Resilience Theory:** Realistic optimism is closely linked to resilience theory, which explores how individuals adapt and thrive in the face of adversity. By maintaining a positive outlook while acknowledging challenges, realistic optimists cultivate resilience and bounce back from setbacks more effectively.

Benefits of Realistic Optimism

Research has identified several benefits associated with adopting a realistic optimistic mindset:

- **Emotional Resilience:** Realistic optimists are better equipped to cope with stress, setbacks, and challenges due to their proactive and problem-solving approach.

- **Improved Mental Health:** Studies suggest that realistic optimism is associated with lower levels of depression, anxiety, and psychological distress.

- **Enhanced Well-being:** Realistic optimists report higher levels of life satisfaction, happiness, and overall well-being compared to pessimists or individuals with rigidly positive attitudes.

- **Health Outcomes:** Research indicates that realistic optimism is linked to better physical health outcomes, such as lower cardiovascular risk and improved immune function.

Neuroscientific Insights

Neuroscience provides insights into how realistic optimism influences brain function and structure:

- **Neuroplasticity:** The brain's ability to reorganize and adapt in response to experience and learning supports the development of realistic optimism through repeated practice and positive reinforcement.

- **Neurochemicals:** Positive emotions associated with realistic optimism, such as hope and satisfaction, are linked to the release of neurotransmitters like dopamine and serotonin, promoting a sense of well-being and motivation.

Practical Applications

This chapter discusses practical strategies for cultivating realistic optimism based on scientific research:

- **Mindfulness and Positive Reframing:** Practicing mindfulness to observe and reframe negative thoughts into more realistic and constructive perspectives.

- **Goal Setting and Action Planning:** Setting SMART goals (Specific, Measurable, Achievable, Relevant, Time-bound) and developing action plans to achieve them while anticipating potential obstacles.

- **Social Support and Resilience Building:** Building strong social connections and seeking support from others during challenging times to enhance resilience and maintain optimism.

Case Studies and Examples

Case studies and real-life examples illustrate how individuals have applied realistic optimism in various contexts, such as career advancement, health challenges, and personal relationships. These stories demonstrate the transformative power of realistic optimism in fostering resilience, perseverance, and personal growth.

In conclusion, realistic optimism is not just a philosophical approach but a scientifically validated mindset that promotes emotional resilience, well-being, and adaptive coping strategies. By understanding its psychological foundations and incorporating evidence-based practices into daily life, individuals can cultivate a balanced perspective, navigate challenges effectively, and lead more fulfilling lives.

CHAPTER TEN

Applying Realistic Optimism in Everyday Life

In the final chapter, we offer practical tips and exercises for integrating realistic optimism into daily routines and overcoming common obstacles. We emphasize the ongoing nature of personal growth and provide guidance on sustaining a positive mindset in various life situations.

Realistic optimism is a powerful mindset that can be applied across various aspects of daily life to enhance well-being, foster resilience, and achieve personal goals. This chapter explores practical strategies and applications of realistic optimism in everyday situations, offering insights and tools for integrating this mindset into routine activities and challenges.

Setting the Foundation

Before diving into practical applications, this section reinforces the core principles of realistic optimism:

- **Balanced Perspective:** Acknowledging both the positive and negative aspects of situations, while maintaining confidence in one's ability to navigate challenges.
- **Adaptive Thinking:** Using cognitive reframing techniques to reinterpret setbacks and obstacles in a constructive light.
- **Resilience Building:** Cultivating emotional resilience by developing coping strategies and maintaining a proactive approach to adversity.

Applying Realistic Optimism

This chapter provides practical examples and scenarios where realistic optimism can be applied effectively:

- **Career and Professional Development:**
    - **Setting Career Goals:** Using SMART goals to define career objectives and creating action plans with realistic timelines and milestones.
    - **Handling Setbacks:** Viewing job rejections or setbacks as opportunities for growth and learning, rather than personal failures.
    - **Networking and Building Relationships:** Maintaining a positive outlook during networking events and professional interactions, focusing on mutual benefits and opportunities.

- **Health and Wellness:**
  - o **Health Challenges:** Facing health challenges with realistic optimism by adhering to treatment plans, maintaining a healthy lifestyle, and seeking support from healthcare professionals.
  - o **Physical Fitness:** Setting achievable fitness goals and celebrating progress, while adapting routines to accommodate fluctuations in energy and motivation.
  - o **Mind-Body Connection:** Practicing mindfulness and stress management techniques to promote overall well-being and resilience.
- **Personal Relationships:**
  - o **Communication and Conflict Resolution:** Approaching conflicts with empathy and understanding,

while seeking constructive solutions that respect individual perspectives.

- o **Friendships and Social Connections:** Nurturing meaningful relationships by appreciating the strengths of others and maintaining realistic expectations.
- o **Family Dynamics:** Balancing familial responsibilities with self-care and boundary-setting, fostering mutual respect and emotional support.

- **Financial Management:**
  - o **Budgeting and Savings Goals:** Adopting a realistic approach to financial planning, setting achievable savings goals, and making informed decisions based on current circumstances.
  - o **Investment and Risk Management:** Evaluating investment opportunities with a balanced perspective on

potential risks and rewards, while seeking professional advice when necessary.

- o **Adapting to Economic Changes:** Adjusting financial strategies in response to economic fluctuations or unexpected expenses, while maintaining a long-term focus on financial security.

Practical Strategies and Techniques

This section offers practical strategies for integrating realistic optimism into everyday life:

- **Gratitude Practice:** Cultivating gratitude for small achievements and positive experiences, fostering a positive mindset.
- **Visualization and Goal Setting:** Using visualization techniques to imagine successful outcomes and setting realistic

goals aligned with personal values and aspirations.

- **Self-Reflection and Learning:** Reflecting on experiences, identifying lessons learned, and applying insights to future endeavors.

- **Flexibility and Adaptability:** Embracing uncertainty and adapting plans when necessary, while remaining resilient in the face of unforeseen challenges.

Case Studies and Success Stories

Illustrative case studies and success stories highlight individuals who have applied realistic optimism to overcome adversity, achieve personal milestones, and cultivate resilience in various aspects of life. These narratives demonstrate the transformative impact of adopting a positive yet grounded mindset.

In conclusion, integrating realistic optimism into everyday life empowers individuals to navigate challenges with resilience, maintain a positive outlook, and achieve meaningful goals. By applying practical strategies and embracing a balanced perspective, individuals can cultivate personal growth, foster supportive relationships, and enhance overall well-being. The principles discussed in this chapter provide a foundation for continued exploration and application of realistic optimism in pursuit of a fulfilling and purposeful life.

Conclusion: Embracing Realistic Optimism

We summarize key insights from the book and encourage readers to embrace the principles of realistic optimism as a pathway to greater resilience, fulfillment, and genuine positivity in their lives.

Appendices

- Additional Resources and Further Reading: Recommended books, articles, and websites for deeper exploration.
- Worksheets and Exercises for Practicing Realistic Optimism: Practical tools to help readers apply concepts discussed in the book to their own lives.

Author's Note

As the author, I believe that by rethinking traditional notions of positive thinking and embracing realistic optimism, individuals can cultivate a more balanced and sustainable approach to personal growth and well-being. I invite readers to embark on this journey of exploration and transformation with an open mind and a willingness to embrace change. Together, let's redefine what it means to think positively and live authentically.